Judaism and Mental Health

Beliefs, Research and Applications

Harold G. Koenig, M.D.

DEDICATION

To those affected by the Holocaust

CONTENTS

INTRODUCTION

This little book is for researchers and anyone interested in the relationship between Judaism and mental health, as well as for mental health professionals and clergy who treat and care for Jewish people with emotional issues. To my knowledge, this is one of the few *evidence-based* sources that briefly and succinctly describe what Jews believe and how it relates to their mental health. The research on Jewish beliefs and practices and mental health is thoroughly and systematically reviewed here, and practical recommendations are provided on how to apply this to the care of Jewish patients and members of Jewish congregations. Please join me in learning more about what Jews believe and practice, how this relates to their mental health and well-being, and what this means for caregivers helping Jews to achieve a full and overcoming life.

Jews make up 0.2% of the world's population (approximately 14 million) (Pew Research Center, 2012). More than one-third of Jews worldwide live in the United States (U.S.) (5.3 million) (2% of U.S. population) and one-third to one-half live in Israel (6.4 million) (Pew Research Center, 2013; Central Bureau of Statistics, 2016). While members of the Jewish faith make up only a small proportion of the earth's population, they have made enormous contributions to medicine -- especially psychiatry and the mental health system in the U.S. and around the world. Sigmund Freud (1856-1939) (psychoanalysis), Abraham Low (1891-1954) (self-help groups for the mentally ill), Viktor Frankl (1905-1997) (importance of meaning), Alfred Adler (1870-1937) (individual psychology and inferiority complex), Albert Ellis (1913-2007) (rational-emotive therapy), Erich Fromm (1900-1980) (theories of personality and political insight), Lawrence Kohlberg (moral development) (1927-1987), Abraham Maslow (1908-1970) (hierarchy of needs), David Wechsler (1896-1981) (intelligence testing), and Joseph Wolpe (1915-1997) (systematic desensitization) were all Jewish. The same is true for many psychiatrists, psychologists, and counselors in the U.S. today.

In the most recent survey of 258 members of the American Psychological Association, 23% were Jewish (Delaney et al., 2013), similar to the 24% reported in an earlier survey of a national sample of U.S. psychologists (Bergin & Jensen, 1990). A survey of 262 members of the Association for Behavioraland Cognitive Therapies (ABCT) reported that 22% were Jewish (Rosmarin et al., 2013). Thus, nearly one-quarter of mental health professionals in the U.S. are Jewish, compared to 2% of the general public.

1 ABOUT JUDAISM

Judaism is about culture, heredity, and religion. This book focuses on the religious elements of Judaism. Here I describe the Sacred Jewish Scriptures and the branches of Judaism that to some extent are determined by the degree to which these sacred scriptures are followed.

Jewish Scriptures

The traditional authoritative scriptures of the Jewish faith tradition are the Tanakh (Hebrew Bible) and the Talmud.

Tanakh. The Tanakh includes the Torah (first five books of the Hebrew Bible also called the Pentateuch), the Nevi'im (books of the prophets[1]), and the Ketuvim (the other books[2]). The Tanakh is comparable to the Christian "Old Testament." The Torah portion of the Tanakh is the most revered of all and is the basis for the Jewish faith.

Talmud. The other sacred scripture is the Talmud (of which the Mishnah is a part). The Mishnah (sometimes referred to as the "oral Torah") describes Jewish life during the Second Temple period

---

[1] Book of Joshua, Book of Judges, 1st and 2nd Samuel, 1st and 2nd Kings, and a single book that contains the major prophets (Isaiah, Jeremiah, Ezekiel) and the minor prophets (Hosea, Joel, Amos, Obadiah, Jonah, Micah, Nahum, Habakkuk, Zephaniah, Haggai, Zechariah, Malachi)

[2] Psalms, Proverbs, Job, Song of Songs, Book of Ruth, Book of Lamentations, Ecclesiastes, Book of Esther, Daniel, Ezra-Nehemiah, Chronicles

(between 530 BCE and 70 CE) and describes Jewish laws that were written down by Rabbi Yehudah Hanasi in the 2nd century CE. The Mishnah is divided into six parts and 63 volumes: Zeraim (agricultural laws), Moed (laws regarding the Sabbath and festival feasts), Nashim (family law, marriage, divorce), Neziquin (civil/criminal laws), Qodashim (laws regarding sacrifices and diet), and Tohorot (laws guiding rituals dealing with defilement and purification). The Mishnah also includes six chapters of wise sayings regarding ethics and interpersonal relationships (Pirkei Avot, i.e., Ethics of the Fathers). Other parts of the Talmud were written later (500 CE) and involve commentaries on the Mishnah (called the Gemara). The Midrash is both a mode of biblical interpretation of the "written" Torah and a literature in itself with ethical and legal sections. The Midrash is referred to extensively in the Gemara. The Mishnah and Gemara together make up the Talmud (or Talmudic literature).

The Talmud was compiled in two versions, the Palestinian and the Babylonian. While there is much overlap between the two, the Babylonian version is often considered the definitive source of Jewish law by scholars today (see discussion by Dimitrovsky, 2001). Orthodox Jews today focus on the study of the Talmud, as do many Conservative Jews.

Branches of Judaism

As with other world religions, there is a wide range of belief among Jews depending on the particular branch of Judaism they ascribe to.

United States. In the U.S., the four major branches of Judaism are Secular, Reform, Conservative, and Orthodox (and Modern Orthodox).

Secular Jews are not religious or observant, but may celebrate traditional Jewish holidays as cultural or historical occasions. Births, deaths, and marriages are secular and do not include religious rituals. Well-known secular Jews in the past were Sigmund Freud, Albert Einstein, and Karl Marx. In the U.S., 90% of Jews consider themselves non-Orthodox (no denomination, reform, conservative, or other). Of American Jews, 30% report no denomination (i.e., considered Secular Jews) (Pew Research Center, 2013).

As a group, *Reform Jews* (sometimes known as Liberal or Progressive Jews) are pluralistic and independent, and tend to oppose any fixed set of beliefs or practices (Petuchowski, 1998). Instead, they prefer to view religious beliefs as changing or evolving with the times, and emphasize ethical values rather than ceremonies and rituals (compared to Conservative or Orthodox Jews). Reform Judaism has from the beginning in the 19th century tended to distance itself from the oral tradition (Encyclopedia Britannica, 2008), although more recently there have been efforts by Reform leaders to reconnect to the Talmud (Dimitrovsky, 2001). Most Reform Jews live in the U.S., where 35% of American Jews indicate this preference (Pew Research Center, 2013).

Conservative Jews seek to preserve the traditional beliefs and rituals of Judaism, but are not as strict in their adherence to the Jewish law as are Orthodox believers. Conservative Jews tend to preserve Jewish traditions, rather than reform or abandon them. However, while being committed to the rabbinic tradition, they believe that Jewish religious laws derived from the oral and written tradition can change based on changing conditions in society (Encyclopedia Britannica, 1998a). Conservative Jews make up about 18% of American Jews (Pew Research Center, 2013). Conservative Jews believe in a personal God and Creator, and may be more critical of the Talmud compared to Orthodox Jews.

Orthodox Jews adhere tightly to the traditional beliefs, practices, and rituals of historical Judaism (Halakhah). Beliefs and practices are those described in the Torah, codified in the Mishnah, and interpreted in the Gemara, and are believed to be as relevant today for guiding life and behavior as they were two millennia ago (Encyclopedia Britannica, 1998b). Orthodox believers make up 10% of Jews in the U.S. Orthodox Jews often engage in worship on a daily basis, comply with kosher dietary habits, pray and conduct religious rituals in a traditional manner, and believe in the intensive study of the Torah and Talmud. Synagogues typically separate men and women, and no musical instruments are allowed during services. There is also a Neo-Orthodox movement in Judaism (sometimes called "Modern Orthodoxy") that dates back to the late 19th century. Modern Orthodox Jews make up about 3% of America Jews overall and 30% of Orthodox American Jews (Pew Research Center, 2016a).

Israel. Over 80% the population of Israel consider themselves Jewish, half (40%) describe themselves as Secular, 23% as Traditional, 10% as Religious, and 8% as Ultra-Orthodox (Pew

Research Center, 2016b). Few Jews in Israel identify themselves as "Reform" (3%) or "Conservative" (2%) as in the U.S. One reason is that the Reform and Conservative traditions developed in Europe and North America, whereas Secular (Hiloni), Traditional (Masorti), Religious (Dati), and Ultra-Orthodox (Haredi) groups emerged from Israel (Pew Research Center, 2016a). These branches of Judaism in Israel compare to some degree (but not entirely) with those in the U.S. Secular Jews in the U.S. are similar to the Hiloni branch in Israel, Reform Jews similar to the Masorti branch, Conservative Jews similar to the Dati branch, and Orthodox Jews similar to the Ultra-Orthodox branch. Again, these are only approximations.

2 CORE JEWISH BELIEFS

As noted earlier (and true for other world religions as well), it is difficult to identify beliefs that are common to all Jews. Maimonides (Rabbi Moses ben Maimon, 1135-1204 CE) was a physician,[3] astronomer, Sephardic Jewish philosopher, and one of the most influential Torah scholars of his time (the Middle Ages). During this period, Maimonides came up with 13 principles (Holzer 1901; Kellner 1980) that have become the most widely accepted fundamental beliefs of the Jewish religious faith ("which every Jew qua Jew had to accept" [Kellner, 1987, p 299]). Despite this claim, however, there has been anything but uniform agreement on these 13 principles (see critique by Shapiro, 1993). The principles are:

(1) G-d exists, is perfect, and is the primary cause of everything that exists

(2) G-d is one and is entirely and completely one, without division and without competition

(3) G-d does not have a body, and therefore does not get tired, need rest, or require some place to live

(4) G-d existed prior to everything else and is eternal

(5) One must worship G-d only and have no false gods (the 1st

---

[3] Maimonides is responsible for the Oath of Maimonides and the Prayer of Maimonides, which are sometimes used by medical schools instead of the Hippocratic Oath upon student graduation

Commandment) or to pray to anyone besides G-d (no intercessors)

(6) G-d communicates through the prophets, and all words of the prophets are true

(7) Moses was the greatest prophet who ever lived (either before or after him)

(8) The Torah is divine, has its origins in heaven, and is the same Torah that was given to Moses

(9) Nothing can ever be subtracted from the Torah, changed in it, or added to it; the Torah is the only law that G-d will ever give to humanity

(10) G-d knows all the deeds of humans

(11) G-d will reward or punish humans based on their compliance with what has been laid down in the Torah

(12) The Messiah ('anointed one,' savior or liberator of the Jewish people) will someday come and issue in the messianic age

(13) All persons who have died will be resurrected some day

In his commentary on the Mishnah in Sanhedrin 10, Maimonides says (at the end of these 13 principles):

> "When all these foundations are perfectly understood and believed in by a person, he enters the community of Israel, and one is obligated to love and pity him and to act towards him in all ways in which the Creator has commanded that one should act towards his brother, with love and fraternity. Even when he to commit every possible transgression, because of lust and because of being overpowered by the evil inclination, he will be punished according to his rebelliousness, but he has a portion [in the world to come]; he is one of the sinners in Israel. But if a man doubts any of these foundations, he leaves the community [of Israel], denies the fundamental, and is called a sectarian, an *epiqoros*, and one who 'cuts among the plantings.' One is required to hate him and destroy him. About such a person it was said, 'Do I not hate them, 0 Lord, who hate Thee?' (Ps. 139:21)." (p 300, translated in Kellner, 1987)

This last controversial statement by Maimonides even calls into question the definition of what it means to be a Jew or at least a religious Jew (traditional and rabbinic Judaism defines a Jew as one who is born of a Jewish mother or one who properly converts to Judaism). According to Menachem Kellner (1987), chair of the Department of Jewish History at University of Haifa, those who adopt these 13 principles are "thereby rendered worthy of all the benefits of being a Jew" (p 300).

These 13 principles come from the Middle-Ages. To what extent do these principles apply to Jews today? Do any modern Jewish scholars hold such beliefs? David Wolpe appears to be one of them. Wolpe, named the most influential rabbi in America by Newsweek Magazine in 2012, writes about Jewish belief in God in very personal terms that reflect the 13 principles above. In an article published in *The Tablet* (one of the most widely read American Jewish magazines in print today), he begins with a description of the love relationship between God and Moses and how this represents the love relationship between God and the Jewish people (Wolpe, 2013). He notes that during Shema (morning and evening prayer services), which he describes as a "love-saturated liturgy," Jews say "With eternal love, You have loved the house of Israel." Wolpe says that God's love is "sewn into the fabric of the universe," and that Jewish tradition holds that the Song of Solomon is all about the love between God and Israel. Such deep belief in and love for God is not a theological view limited to Wolpe alone (see *Star of Redemption* by Franz Rozenzweig [2004], one of the greatest contributors to Jewish philosophy in the twentieth century).

When referring to the traditional core Jewish beliefs and belief in God's love for the Jewish people, some mention of the Holocaust is necessary. The reason is that many Jews were affected by this unfathomable and horrific event. The Jews according to Deuteronomy 14:2 are God's "chosen people."[4] If so, how does one explain the nearly 6 million were murdered during the Holocaust from 1933 to 1945? Many men, women and children suffered terribly during their last days from beatings, torture, exhaustion, starvation, or incineration in the furnaces. If a loving and caring God existed, one who is in control, how could he let this happen? The senselessness of that event, I believe, is one reason why many Jews today no longer believe in God and why Europe moved so rapidly

---

[4] "For thou art a holy people unto HaShem thy G-d, and HaShem hath chosen thee to be His own treasure out of all peoples that are upon the face of the earth." (Jewish Publication Society Bible, 1917)

towards secularization in the latter half of the 20th century. The emotional wounds from the Holocaust continue to impact the mental health of the children and grandchildren of those involved in this tragedy.

3 JEWISH BELIEFS AND PRACTICES

Core Jewish religious beliefs and practices, as with other religious faiths, may not be those that current day Jews in Israel or the United States actually believe or engage in. Systematic surveys of Jews in these countries provide objective information in this regard, which is important for mental health professionals to know about before assuming that certain beliefs or practices are relevant to Jewish patients.

Beliefs and Practices in Israel

The Pew Research Center is the most reliable and recent source of information about Jews today. The following data are based on a random survey of 3,789 Jewish adults living in Israel (Pew Research Center, 2016b).

Beliefs. Half (50%) of Israeli Jews say they believe in God with absolute certainty (94% of Ultra-Orthodox and Religious compared to 37% of Traditional and Secular). Similarly, 61% indicate that God gave Israel to the Jewish people (99% of Ultra-Orthodox/Religious vs. 51% of Traditional/Secular). Less than one-third (30%), however, say that religion is "very important" in their lives (90% of Ultra-Orthodox/Religious vs. 13% of Traditional/Secular).

Practices. Practices also depend heavily on the branch of Judaism that is ascribed to. Concerning weekly or more often study of the Torah or Gemara, all (100%) Ultra-Orthodox Jews do so compared to only 1% of Secular Jews. Overall, 21% of Israeli Jews study the Torah/Gemara at least weekly. Three-quarters (76%) of

Ultra-Orthodox Jews pray at least daily, compared to only 1% of Secular Jews. Likewise, 85% of Ultra-Orthodox Jews attend religious services at least weekly compared to 1% of Secular Jews (overall, 27% of Israeli Jews).

With regard to handling money on the Sabbath, almost all Ultra-Orthodox Jews (>99%) say that they avoid doing so. In contrast, only a small percentage of Secular Jews say they do not handle money on the Sabbath (12%). Likewise, most Ultra-Orthodox Jews (>99%) avoid driving a car or riding on a train or bus on the Sabbath, whereas only 5% of Secular Jews do not travel on the Sabbath. Overall, 41% of Israeli Jews avoid handling money and 35% avoid traveling on the Sabbath. With regard to fasting on Yom Kippur (the most important Jewish holy day, when Jews ask forgiveness for their sins and seek atonement), 99% of Ultra-Orthodox Jews fast the entire day, whereas only 30% of Secular Jews do so. Overall, 60% of Israeli Jews fast the entire day and 27% do not fast at all.

With regard to Jewish men wearing a head covering (either a crocheted kippa or black fabric kippa), 100% of Ultra-Orthodox Jews wear such head coverings (53% wear a large black kippa) but only 36% of Israeli Jews overall do so. Few Jewish women wear head coverings (19%) unless they are Ultra-Orthodox (93%). Most Israeli Jews (70%) usually or always light candles on Hanukkah, which is an 8-day period commemorating the rededication of the Temple after its desecration in 165 BCE; even 45% of Secular Jews do light candles on Hanukkah. Likewise, most Jews in Israel (93%) say they held or attended a Seder, i.e., an evening gathering of friends and family for dinner. This practice commemorates the first day of Passover when the Israelites were liberated from slavery in Egypt; most Secular Jews (87%) also hold or attend a Passover Seder. However, much fewer said they attended a "traditional" Passover Seder (67% of all Israeli Jews and 41% of Secular Jews), which involves a meal with special foods and a ceremony that includes religious rituals and prayers, reading of commentaries from the Talmud, and singing of Passover songs.

Finally, there are Jewish dietary practices. These involve keeping Kosher, i.e., adhering to traditional Jewish dietary laws (kashrut) such as avoiding pork and shellfish and not including meat and dairy products in the same meal. Nearly two-thirds (63%) of Israeli Jews overall say they keep Kosher at home, including 100% of Ultra-

Orthodox Jews and 33% of Secular Jews. Somewhat fewer Israeli Jews keep Kosher outside the home (52%), except for Ultra-Orthodox Jews (100%). Even 67% of Secular Jews, however, do not eat pork.

Sephardi Jews (those who are descended from Jews living in the Iberian Peninsula, i.e., Spain/Portugal, around 1000 CE) and Mizrahi Jews (descended from local Jewish communities in the Middle East since biblical times) are more likely to engage in these traditional Jewish practices than Ashkenazi Jews (those descended from Jews originating in Eastern Europe).

Beliefs and Practices in the United States

The following information on American Jews is based on a random national sample of 3,475 Jewish adults, including 2,786 Jews who claim a religion and 689 Jews who claim no religion (Pew Research Center, 2013).

Beliefs. Overall, American Jews tend to be less religious than Israeli Jews. This is especially true for those who are not Orthodox. More than one out of five (22%) report they have no religion, 30% indicate no religious denomination, over 60% say that being Jewish is primarily a matter of their ancestry and culture, and two-thirds (68%) say that you don't have to believe in God to be Jewish. Among Orthodox Jews, 89% say they believe in God with absolute certainty, compared to 41% of Conservative Jews, 29% of Reform Jews, and 18% of Secular Jews. While 20% of Reform Jews and 39% of Secular Jews indicated that they do not believe in God, Silverman and colleagues (2016) commenting on this finding say that belief in God among Jews is "complex" and needs a more nuanced discussion.

Most Orthodox Jews (84%) believe that God gave Israel to the Jewish people, compared to 35% of non-Orthodox Jews (40% for all American Jews). Likewise, 83% of Orthodox Jews say that religion in very important in their lives, compared to 43% of Conservative Jews, 16% of Reform Jews, and 8% of Secular Jews (26% for all American Jews). Most say that what is essential to being Jewish involves remembering the Holocaust (73%) and leading an ethical/moral life (69%). Interestingly, 34% of American Jews say that belief in Jesus as the messiah is compatible with being Jewish (46% of Secular Jews say this). Only 19% of American Jews say that to be Jewish means observing the Jewish Law.

Practices. Traditional Jewish practices are also less common in American Jews than they are in Israeli Jews. Among Orthodox Jewish Americans, 74% say they attend religious services at least monthly, compared to 38% of Conservative, 17% of Reform, and 6% of Secular Jews (11% for all American Jews). Less than one-third of American Jews (31%) are even members of a synagogue.

The practice of not handling money on the Sabbath is followed by 78% of Orthodox Jews compared to only 8% of non-Orthodox (15% for all American Jews). With regard to keeping Kosher at home, 92% of Orthodox Jews do so compared to 31% of Conservative, 7% of Reform, and 10% of Secular Jews (22% for all American Jews). Nearly two-thirds (65%) of non-Orthodox Jews eat pork. Fasting all day long on Yom Kippur is likewise prevalent among Orthodox Jews (94%) but less so (34%) among non-Orthodox (40% for all American Jews). Finally, holding or attending a Passover Seder is prevalent among both Orthodox (99%) and non-Orthodox (66%) Jews.

Relationship to Mental Health

Given the beliefs and practices above, what effects might Jewish beliefs and practices have on mental health? These are likely dependent on the particular branch of Judaism that one ascribes to. With regard to positive effects, religious Jews (those affiliated with Orthodox or Conservative branches) are likely to experience the positive benefits that religious faith and practice often provide (Koenig et al., 2012). Most American Jews (75%), especially Orthodox (99%) and Conservative Jews (92%) report a strong sense of belonging to the Jewish people, i.e., the Jewish community (Pew Research Center, 2013). This connection is likely enhanced by engaging in traditional religious practices and rituals. A strong sense of community is likely to benefit mental health by enhancing the availability of social support when needed, thus helping individuals cope better with life stressors. This is likely to be true for religious Jews who attend synagogue regularly. Being certain that God exists (and that God is loving and persona) may also benefit believing Jews by enhancing a divine relationship that provides meaning and purpose to life, especially during times of loss, change, or illness.

One might also speculate about adverse effects on mental health. Given the large proportion of American Jews (30%) and Israeli Jews

(40%) who considered themselves secular, the mental health of this group is likely to be similar to others with no religious affiliation or interest. Given the expanding evidence base that suggests religious involvement is good for mental health, the mental health of secular Jews may not be comparable to that of religious Jews (possibly increasing risk of depression, suicide, and other emotional disorders), particularly among those who are disconnected from the Jewish community. On the other end of the spectrum, Orthodox Judaism (which may encourage rigid and inflexible following of the oral and written Jewish law) may lead to or conceal obsessive/compulsive religious practices. Given their minority status within Judaism, Orthodox Jews may also experience discrimination by other Jews or by non-Jews who view them as strange or different. Finally, given Orthodox Jews' adherence to traditional Jewish ways of dealing with mental illness, there may be reluctance to seek out secular mental health care when needed. The high prevalence of Jews among mental health professionals, however, may compensate for this tendency (particularly among Reform and Secular Jews).

The possible connections with mental health suggested above are pure speculation. Only systematic research can verify such claims. Thus, an examination of research that (a) compares the mental health of Jews with the mental health of non-Jews and (b) examines the relationship between religiosity and mental health within Jewish populations may help to clarify connections between Judaism and either positive or negative mental health. Summarized in the next few chapters will be studies identified from a systematic review of the literature that examined research conducted prior to 2010 (*Past Research*) (Koenig et al., 2012). I will also review selected studies that illustrate the kind of research conducted since 2010 (*Recent Research*) based on a non-systematic review of the best studies conducted in the last 7 years (CSTH, 2010-2017). These chapters focus on religious coping, depression, suicide, anxiety, substance abuse, and psychological well-being.

4 RELIGIOUS COPING

Religious coping involves the use of religious beliefs and practices to cope with and make sense of traumatic life stressors, and is one of the main reasons for expecting a relationship between religiosity and mental health in Jews.

Past Research

In a small mixed-methods study, Goodman et al (1991) interviewed 12 elderly Jewish and 17 elderly non-Jewish (Protestant or Catholic) women in Philadelphia (USA) who were coping with the loss of an adult child. The interviews revealed that Jewish women tended to be depressed and fixed in their grief, with the loss continuing to be central in their lives. In contrast, non-Jewish women showed signs of acceptance and moving on. Quantitative analyses indicated that positive affect was lower, and depression and loneliness higher in Jewish compared to non-Jewish women. Investigators explained (p S328):

> "The belief that things are in God's hands, that life is preparation for death and that resurrection leads to eternal life (Livingston, 1989) may be instrumental in easing the burden of loss for non-Jewish women. For Jews, rewards and punishments are dispensed in *this* life, with attribution for life's joys and sorrows a matter of individual interpretation rather than "the will of God" (Kushner, 1981). Left to their own interpretations, Jewish women may have seen their loss as something they could

have prevented or as punishment for their own failures in life or shortcomings as mothers. A lingering sense of guilt or the Jewish reverence for suffering (Frankl, 1963) would make grief a permanent fixture in their lives and account for the depression we encountered."

At the other end of the age spectrum, Dubow and colleagues (2000) surveyed 75 synagogue-attending Jewish adolescents (average age 12.6 years) in a Midwestern US city. The primary stressors faced by these young participants were deciding on whether to go to a Hebrew school, being unable to do things they wanted because of having to attend Shabbat or other Jewish holidays, worrying over their Bar/Bat Mitzvah, and dealing with other kids making anti-Semitic comments about them (more than 50% of adolescents indicated each of these). Researchers attributed this to the tension between cultural assimilation and the maintenance of Jewish tradition. The most common behaviors used to cope with these stressors were doing good deeds (51%), asking God for forgiveness (43%), spending time with Jewish friends (41%), and praying for God's love and care (27%). The authors concluded that Jewish adolescents often both struggle with religious issues and depend on religion to cope with those stressors.

Solomon and colleagues (2005) surveyed a random sample of 512 adults in Israel (87% Jewish and 46% non-religious). A single item to assess coping by faith in God. The majority indicated they coped by faith in God (60%). Among women, faith in God was reported to be the most effective coping strategy of all the different coping behaviors that were assessed (86% of women indicated this).

With regard to locus of control concerning health (LOC), Cohen and Azaiza (2007) surveyed a random population-based sample of 358 Jews and 162 Arabs ages 50-75 years living in Israel, finding that Jews were more likely than Arabs to have an internal health LOC (good) and less likely to have an external LOC (bad), controlling for gender. However, this may have resulted from the way "internal" and "external" LOC were measured. Having an external LOC may have been perceived by Arabs as placing trust and control in God's hands, rather than depending on themselves to control health outcomes. Arabs were considerably more religious than were Jews in this sample.

Recent Research

Pirutinsky et al (2012) examined the relationship between religious coping, obesity, and emotional functioning in 212 Jews from Orthodox, Conservative, and Reform traditions in the U.S. and Canada via an Internet survey (average age of participants was 42 years). Positive emotional functioning was assessed using a standard 12-item scale and religious coping by the 12-item Jewish Religious Coping Scale (JCOPE). Uncontrolled correlations indicated that weight (body mass index or BMI) and emotional functioning were inversely correlated (r=-0.20, p<0.005), i.e., those with a higher BMI had significantly worse emotional functioning. Religious coping was unrelated to either emotional functioning or BMI. However, among those who scored *low on positive religious coping*, BMI was strongly and inversely correlated with emotional functioning (B= -0.32, p<0.001), whereas among those who scored *high on positive religious coping*, the relationship between BMI and emotional functioning was not significant (B=+0.03, p=0.78). After controlling for age, smoking, physical health, and level of physical activity, the buffering effect of religious coping on BMI and emotional functioning actually increased in strength.

Rokach et al (2012) examined differences in "coping with loneliness" between Secular (n=28), Conservative (n=54), and Orthodox Jews (n=168) living in Israel (average age 39 years). A 34-item six subscale loneliness questionnaire examined behaviors used to cope with loneliness: (1) reflection and acceptance, (2) self-development and understanding, (3) social support network, (4) distancing and denial, (5) increased activity (alone or in a group), and (6) religion and faith. Religion and faith were assessed by five items that measured "need to connect to and worship a Divine entity" through prayer and religious attendance. After controlling for age, sex, and marital status, results indicated no differences between secular, conservative, and orthodox Jews on ways of coping with loneliness (except scores on the religion/faith subscale, which was -- as expected -- higher in Conservative and Orthodox Jews).

Many Secular Jews in Israel consult Orthodox rabbis on issues related to health matters, treating sick children, breast cancer, treatments for infertility, pre-natal testing, pregnancy, spiritual healing, genetic counseling, and mental health care. The cause of this has remained a mystery. Keshet and Liberman (2014) conducted qualitative semi-structured open-ended interviews with 50 non-religious Jews living in the Western Galilee region of Israel to discuss this issue. Interviewees said they expected the rabbi to (a) tell them if the medical procedure would succeed, (b) provide emotional support, (c) help them make difficult decisions, (d) give blessings for success, cure or health, and even (e) help with practical needs. The rabbi was chosen based on his reputation for performing miracles, or expertise in a particular area such as interpersonal relations, romantic attachments, fertility problems, or other health-related problems. Most of rabbis were from North Africa and were masters in Jewish mysticism, i.e., Kabbalah. Many were believed to possess divine grace that they inherited from ancestors. Some rabbis were believed to possess extraordinary powers to diagnose problems. Treatments often involved the rabbi praying for and blessing them, suggesting they change the name of a sick child, using amulets for healing, and telling them to read sections of the Psalms, the Kabbalistic Zohar, or visit the graves of holy persons. Most interviewees said they were not required to pay for treatment, but were encouraged to provide a small donation ranging from $14 to $50. Researchers concluded that non-religious Jews consulted rabbis because this was a source of "culture-based empowerment."

Summary
Although religious coping may be different in Jews compared to Christians and Muslims, it is not uncommon for Jews (including adolescents) to rely on God when attempting to cope with stress. Indeed, the largest and best-designed study to date indicates that more than half of Jews in Israel do so (Solomon et al., 2005). Not surprisingly, this is especially true for those who are religious or Orthodox. Even Secular Jews in Israel consult rabbis to assist them in coping with health problems and life stress. Positive religious coping and intrinsic religiosity, however, also appear to buffer against the effects of stressors (e.g., physical health problems, obesity) on emotional functioning in American Jews. Jews in Israel are more likely to have an *internal* locus of control compared to Arabs, although the reasons for this are not clear (and may be because Arabs are more likely to put control in God's hands, which can be viewed as an *external* locus of control).

5 DEPRESSION

Depression is the most common and disabling mental disorder in the world, and according to the Harvard School of Public Health and World Health Organization, is projected in 2020 to be second only to ischemic heart disease in the cause of disability-adjusted life years (Murray & Lopez, 1996, p 4; Lopez & Murray, 1998). At least 14 studies have compared Jews and non-Jews on depressive symptoms and disorder, or have examined whether religious Jews are more or less depressed than secular Jews.

Past Research
In one of the first U.S. studies to compare depression in Jews and non-Jews, Figelman (1968) compared psychiatric disorders among newly admitted patients to Boston State Hospital (70 African-Americans and 36 Jewish Americans). Disorders that were compared were paranoid (paranoid delusions or paranoid schizophrenia) and affective disorder (manic depression, psychotic depression, neurotic depression, or affective psychoses). Results indicated a low frequency of paranoid diagnoses but a high frequency of depressive disorders among Jewish patients (72% among Jews vs. 43% among Blacks, p<0.05).

Malzberg (1973) examined the prevalence of depression diagnoses in first admissions to all mental hospitals in the state of New York between 1959 and 1961 (5,514 Jewish and 34,707 non-Jewish whites). Among native born Jews, involutional depression and manic depressive illness were present in 12.1% and 5.8%, compared to 7.5% and 2.5% in non-Jews, respectively. Among those who were foreign born, rates were 18.6% and 3.9% in Jews compared to 10.0% and 1.6% in non-Jews.

Cooklin et al (1983) conducted a case-control study of 786 psychiatric inpatients discharged between 8/1/76 and 12/31/78 from Harrow Hospital in London. Among these patients, 64 Jewish persons were identified by the Jewishness of their name, case notes, and other methods. Diagnoses were compared among Jewish and non-Jewish inpatients, after taking into account age and sex differences. Again, affective psychoses (50% vs 28%, p<.01) and affective disorders overall (66% vs 43%, p<.01) were more common among Jews than non-Jews. Similar findings were reported in a study of 152 psychiatric patients in New York City (Flics & Herron, 1991).

All of the reports above involve psychiatric populations. What about non-psychiatric populations? Yeung and Greenwald (1992) analyzed data on random sample of 3,640 adults participating in the New Haven site of the NIMH Epidemiologic Catchment Area (ECA) study, comparing rates of psychiatric disorder and help seeking behavior in Jews and non-Jews. Again, significantly higher rates of major depression and dysthymia were reported among Jews compared to Catholics and Protestants. Jews were also more likely than non-Jews to seek treatment from mental health specialists and general physicians for their emotional problems. Levav et al (1997) also compared rates of major depression in a random sample of 5,772 adults in Los Angeles and New Haven using ECA data. While no difference was found between Jewish and non-Jewish women, Jewish men had significantly higher rates of major depression than non-Jewish men for both current and lifetime rates. Non-Jewish males were 70% less likely than Jewish males to have current major depression (OR=0.30, 95% CI 0.14-0.62), and 50% less likely to have a lifetime history of major depression (OR=0.50, 95% CI 0.29-0.87).

In one of the few studies that examined participants over time, Kennedy et al (1996) followed 1,855 older community residents (40% Jewish and 47% Catholic) living in the North Bronx area of New York City. Jews were more likely to have seen a mental health professional than Catholics or members of other faiths (3.2% vs 1.4% and 1.8%), more likely to use psychotropic medication (10.8% vs 7.0% and 4.9%), and more likely to score high on the CES-D depression scale (20.7% vs. 9.5% and 12.3%). Using logistic regression to control for other covariates, Jews were 75% more likely than non-Jews to suffer from depression (OR=1.75, 95% CI 1.51-2.01, p<.0001). When followed over 24 months, Jews were also more likely to become depressed than Catholics or members of other religious faiths (50.7% vs 37.3% and 11.9%, a difference that persisted after controlling for six other predictors in a multivariate model) and to have persistent depression if depressed at the start of the study (64.5% vs 27.9% and 7.5%).

What about the relationship between **religiosity and depression** in Jews? Are religious or secular Jews more depressed? In the Kennedy et al (1996) study above, frequent religious attendance was associated with lower rates of depression in Catholics (OR 0.37, 95% CI 0.24-0.56, p<.0001). However, this was not true for Jews. In another study conducted in New York City, Springer and colleagues (2003) surveyed 118 community-dwelling older Jewish adults, examining the relationship between religiosity/spirituality and depression. They used the 7-item INSPIRIT to assess religiosity/spirituality and the Brief Depression Scale to assess depressive symptoms. Again, no association was found.

In a study conducted in Israel, Solomon and colleagues (2005) surveyed a representative sample of the Israeli adult population (n=512, 87% Jewish and 46% non-religious), administering a single item to assess depression and a single item to assess coping by faith in God. Those indicating they coped by faith in God (60%) were significantly *more depressed* than those using other coping behaviors (B=0.14, p<0.01).

Research on the relationship between religiosity and depression among Jews in Canada, however, indicates a different pattern. Rosmarin and colleagues (2009a) conducted two Internet studies involving Canadian Jews. In the first study, 565 community-dwelling Jewish adults in Canada (44% Orthodox) were surveyed via the Internet with a 12-item measure of religious beliefs (focusing on God as a benevolent being) and the 20-item CES-D to assess depressive symptoms. No difference in depression was found between Orthodox and non-Orthodox Jews. However, religiosity was inversely related to depressive symptoms especially among Orthodox Jews (r=-0.32, p<0.001); the association was present but weaker in non-Orthodox Jews (r=-0.13, p<0.05). In the second study, 331 community dwelling Jewish and Christian Canadian adults (141

Orthodox, 93 non-Orthodox, 97 Christian) were surveyed using the same 12-item measure of religious beliefs used in the first study, a 4-item measure of religious practices, and again the 20-item CES-D. As in the first study, religious beliefs and religious practices were inversely correlated with depressive symptoms in Orthodox Jews (r=-0.41, p<0.001. for beliefs; r=-0.32, p<0.001, for practices). The same was true for Protestants (r=-0.32, p<0.01 and r=-0.22, p<0.05, respectively). However, no relationship was found in non-Orthodox Jews (r=-0.16 and r=-0.03, respectively, neither of which were statistically significant).

In a third study, Rosmarin and colleagues (2009b) surveyed 354 community dwelling adults (66% Jewish) living in the U.S. (56%), Canada (28%), and outside North America (16%). Relationships were examined between religious beliefs (5-item scale), practices (4-item scale), and Trust/Mistrust in God (25-item scale). Among Jews, 13 were Hasidic, 37 were Yeshiva Orthodox, 91 were modern Orthodox, 50 were Conservative, and 12 were Reform. Depressive symptoms were lowest in Yeshiva Orthodox (7.1 average CES-D) and Reform (8.6) Jews, and highest in Hassidic (15.9) and Conservative Jews (14.7); however, after controlling for age and gender, significant differences disappeared. In the overall sample (that included 34% Christians), general religiousness, religious practices, and trust in God were all inversely related to depressive symptoms, whereas mistrust in God was positively related to depression (controlling for age and whether receiving treatment).

Recent Research

In a study of 89 Orthodox and 123 non-Orthodox Jews from the U.S. (83%), Canada (7%), Israel (6%), and other countries, Pirutinsky et al (2011) examined the role that religion played in buffering the relationship between chronic medical illness and depression. Chronic medical illness was measured by the SF-12 (higher scores indicating less chronic illness); depressive symptoms were measured with the 10-item CES-D scale; and intrinsic religiosity was assessed with the 3-item intrinsic religiosity subscale of the Duke Religion Index (DUREL). A strong relationship was found between poor physical health and higher depressive symptoms in the overall sample, and a strong inverse relationship was found between religiosity and depressive symptoms (B=-0.57, p<0.001). Among those with low intrinsic religiosity, the relationship between poor physical health and depressive symptoms was strong (B=-0.42, p<0.001), but among those with high intrinsic religiosity, no significant relationship was found between poor physical health and depressive symptoms (B=-0.08, p=0.29). Thus, high intrinsic religiosity completely buffered the effects of poor physical health on depressive symptoms in both Orthodox and non-Orthodox Jews.

Krumrei et al (2013) analyzed data from an Internet survey of 208 Jews (33% Modern Orthodox, 22% Yeshiva Orthodox, 14% Reform, and 2% each Hassidic, Reconstructionist, and Sephardic, and 10% other forms of Judaism; 83% from U.S.). Administered were a 6-item Trust/Mistrust in God scale, the 16-item Jewish Religious Coping scale, and the 3-item intrinsic religiosity subscale of the DUREL. Depressive symptoms were assessed using the 10-item CES-D. Bivariate analyses revealed inverse correlations between all measures of religious involvement and depressive symptoms (r= −0.22 for trust in God, p<0.01; −0.24 for intrinsic religiosity, p<0.01; and −0.26 for positive religious coping, p<0.01). In contrast, positive correlations were found between depressive symptoms and mistrust in God (+0.37, p<0.01) and negative religious coping (+0.38, p<0.01). Controlling for gender and age, the correlations above with depressive symptoms remained robust and significant (p<0.01 to p<0.001).

Feinson and Meir (2015) examined the impact of recalled sexual, physical and/or emotional abuse on the mental health of adult Jewish women attending primary health care clinics in Jerusalem. Participants were 261 Ultra-Orthodox, 181 Modern Orthodox, 167 Traditional, and 181 Secular. Childhood abuse was assessed using a global measure of physical, sexual, or verbal abuse, measuring both abuse as a child and abuse within the past year. Mental health was assessed using the Brief Symptom Inventory (BSI) consisting of three subscales: depression, anxiety, and somatization. The frequency of reported childhood abuse (45.0%) and recent abuse (35.8%) was not significantly different between the four groups. However, mental health based on the total BSI score was better in Ultra-Orthodox and Modern Orthodox women than in Traditional and Secular women (p=0.02), even after controlling for age, marital status, income, and education.

Finally, Ronneberg et al (2016) analyzed data from a 2-year prospective study of 7,732 older adults (mean age 68) participating in the U.S. Health and Retirement Study, a nationally representative survey of adults over age 50 (which included 158 Jews). They found that while religiosity protected participants against depression (assessed by the 8-item CESD) in the overall sample, Jews who were depressed at baseline were more likely to remain depressed at follow-up compared to Catholics (the reference group) (OR=2.1, p=0.04).

Summary

Seven of seven studies (100%) that compared Jews and non-Jews found that Jews experienced more depressive symptoms and depressive disorder than non-Jews. Although most of these studies were cross-sectional, two studies were prospective (both over 24 months), finding that Jews were less likely to recover from depression and more likely to become depressed. The high percentage of secular Jews in these studies may help to explain this trend. All of these studies comparing Jews and non-Jews, however, were conducted either in the U.S. or the United Kingdom (not Israel).

With regard to eight studies that examined the relationship between religiosity and depression in Jews, six (75%) reported less depression among Jews who were more religious. Of those six studies, three found this association in Orthodox Jews only, not in non-Orthodox Jews. Again, the majority of these studies were conducted in Jews from the U.S. or Canada, although two studies were done in Israel, one finding lower depression scores among Ultra-Orthodox and Modern Orthodox women (vs. non-Orthodox), and one finding a positive relationship between coping by faith in God and depression (although this may have resulted from turning to God when experiencing depression). Thus, while Jews tend to suffer from more depression than non-Jews, greater religiosity is related to less depression in the majority of studies conducted in Jews.

6 SUICIDE

Suicide is the most feared consequence of depression, and is strictly forbidden by Orthodox Jewish law based on Genesis 9:5-6[5] (non-Orthodox views are more forgiving, especially among Reform Jewish scholars). Unfortunately, there is little research on this topic in Jewish populations.

Past Research

Bailey and Stein (1995) examined suicide rates by state in the U.S., finding that percentage of the state's population that was Jewish was inversely related to the suicide rate ($r=-0.26$, $p<0.05$), an association that remained significant after controlling for other social predictors of suicide (Lester, 1996). Danto and Danto (1983) also reported lower suicide rates among Jews compared to non-Jews in Oakland County, Michigan (Jews identified by type of funeral and cemetery). In that study, suicide rate among Jews was 6.86 per 100,000 compared to 14.07 per 100,000 among non-Jews. In a study of suicide attempts by children, Garfinkel and colleagues (1982) assessed 505 children and adolescents consecutively admitted over seven years to hospital emergency rooms in Toronto, Canada. They were

---

[5] "And surely your blood of your lives will I require; at the hand of every beast will I require it; and at the hand of man, even at the hand of every man's brother, will I require the life of man. Whoso sheddeth man's blood, by man shall his blood be shed; for in the image of G-d made He man" (Jewish Publication Society Bible, 1917).

compared to 505 controls matched by sex, age, and time admitted to the ER. Suicide attempters were significantly less likely to be Catholic or Jewish, compared to controls (42.7% of cases vs. 52.0% of controls, p<0.05).

These findings contrast to those from one of the earliest studies on record by Gargas (1932), who reported that suicide rates in the Netherlands between 1900 and 1910 in Jews were higher (28.3/100,000) than in either Protestants (17.1/100,000) or Catholics (7.0/100,000). He attributed this to Jewish "participation in the commercial world" (p 710). Likewise, Edland and Duncan (1973) who conducted a case-control study of suicides between 1950 and 1972 in Monroe County (Rochester, New York), found that the suicide rate among Jews on a population-wide basis was twice that of Catholics and Protestants. Levav and Aisenberg (1989) reported that while suicide rates in Israel in the early 1980s were relatively low (7.5/100,000) compared to other countries like the U.S. and Northern Europe, suicide rates among Jews *in Israel* between 1976 and 1985 were significantly higher (averaging 9.5/100,000), especially among European born Jews (15.8/100,000) compared to non-Jews (4.6/100,000) particularly Muslim Arabs (2.9/100,000).

Finally, Stein et al (1992) assessed the relationship between religiosity and suicidal attitudes in a representative sample of 525 Jewish Israeli adolescents age 16-17 years old. Attitudes were measured using a 4-item scale and religiosity was assessed by three religious categories: religious (12%), traditional (34%), and not religious (54%). Those who were not religious were significantly more likely to have positive attitudes toward suicide (p<0.001), independent of gender, father's education, exposure to suicide, suicidal thoughts, suicidal feelings, or life-endangering behavior.

Recent Research

Amit and colleagues (2014) examined a random national sample of 620 Jewish adolescents living in Israel (60% Ultra-Orthodox or observant; 40% non-observant), finding that Ultra-Orthodox or observant adolescents were 55% less likely than non-observant adolescents to engage in self-injurious thoughts and behaviors (OR=0.45, 95% CI 0.20-0.99). Self-injurious thoughts and behaviors were assessed by a structured psychiatric interview and findings were confirmed by a psychiatrist, and the findings were controlled for depression. No other factors significantly predicted suicidal tendencies (including gender, parental marital status, siblings, education of mother, welfare status, paternal unemployment, or immigration status).

Summary
Three studies reported greater suicide rates/attempts in Jews (compared to non-Jews) and three report lower suicide rates. Most of these studies involve Jews from the U.S. and Canada, although the one study conducted in Israel found higher rates in Jews compared to Muslim Arabs (although under-reporting may be a problem in Muslim Arabs due to severe prohibitions against suicide). In the remaining two studies of religiosity and suicide attitudes, both conducted in Israel and in adolescents, religious Jews were significantly less likely to have positive attitudes toward suicide.

7 ANXIETY

Orthodox or religious Jews may feel anxious or guilty over failing to perform religious rituals or being unable to live up to the high moral/ethical standards of the Jewish faith. But what does the research show? Here are the results of 17 systematically identified studies.

Past Research
Florian and Kravetz (1983) surveyed 178 healthy Israeli males ages 18 to 30 (mean 21.5 years, equal numbers of university students, orthodox Jewish religious school students, and military cadets). Researchers assessed fear of death using a six factor scale, and measured religious commitment by the 20-item religious practices subscale of the Jewish Religiosity Index (Ben-Meir & Kedem, 1979). Participants were divided into thirds based on their religious commitment score. In general, little relationship was found between religious commitment and fear of death scales. However, those who were more religious were less likely to fear self-annihilation, but more likely to fear consequences to family and friends and punishment in the hereafter.

Zeidner and Hammer (1992) surveyed 261 Jews (mean age 29) in northern Israel involved in a missile crisis during the Gulf War. The COPE scale (Carver) measured coping strategies, which included "increased engagement in religious activities." Investigators also assessed coping resources, including "spiritual/philosophical" resources. The State-Trait Anxiety Inventory (STAI) (Spielberger) and Personal Stress Symptom Assessment (Numeroff) were also administered. Increased religious coping activities and spiritual/ philosophical resources were correlated with *greater* anxiety (r=0.33, p<.05, and r=.20, p<.05, respectively). Associations persisted after controlling for other variables in regression models. Researchers hypothesized that either (1) those who were more spiritual perceived war as a greater threat to their religious culture, nation, and people, or (2) they turned to religion for comfort during the stress of the missile crisis.

Numerous other cross-sectional studies examined religiosity and anxiety in Jews between 2000 and 2010. These studies focused on obsessive-compulsive (OC) symptoms, obsessive-compulsive disorder (OCD), post-traumatic stress disorder (PTSD) symptoms, and general anxiety symptoms (assessed by Spielberger's STAI).

Greenberg and Shefler (2002) interviewed 28 Ultra-Orthodox Jewish psychiatric patients with OCD in Jerusalem. They found that religious symptoms of the disorder were three times more common than non-religious symptoms, and religious symptoms were described as the main difficulty in more than two-thirds of cases. No difference, however, was found in distress, resistance, sense of irrationality, or hours spent daily between religious and non-religious symptoms. Hermesh et al (2003) compared 22 Israeli psychiatric patients with OCD, 22 patients with panic disorder (PD), and 22 healthy controls matched by sex, age, and referring therapist. Religiosity was assessed with a 43-item version of the Jewish Religiosity Scale (Ben-Meir & Kedem, 1979). Religiosity was significantly lower in PD patients compared to healthy controls (14.0 vs. 27.1, p<0.05). Religiosity in PD patients also tended to be lower than in OCD patients (14.0 vs. 25.7) whose average score was similar to that of healthy controls. In OCD patients, no significant correlations were found between religiosity and OCD symptoms (using the standard Y-BOCS scale), and no significant difference in religiosity was found between OCD patients with religious symptoms and OCD patients with non-religious symptoms.

Zohar et al (2005) conducted two surveys of OCD in Israeli Jews, one study involving 256 university students and the other study involving 61 community-dwelling adults. In the student sample, several OC symptom scales (OCD symptoms, obsessive thoughts, perfectionism) and a 22-item student religiosity scale were administered. Results indicated no association between religiosity and OCD symptoms or obsessive thoughts, and only a weak correlation with perfectionism (r=0.12, p<0.05). While "obsessive thoughts" were more common among those with a conservative religious upbringing than in those with a liberal one, no difference in OCD symptoms was found between these two groups. In a small subgroup of 12 participants who had become *more religious* since childhood, scores on several OC symptom scales were significantly higher than in those who had become less religious (n=24). In the second study, 31 adults who had become *more religious* since childhood were compared to 30 who had become less religious. Again, OC symptoms were more common in those who had become more religious.

Hyman (2005) compared PTSD symptoms between religious and non-religious groups of Israeli Jewish body handlers who were working side-by-side (body handlers collect body parts after terrorist attacks, car accidents, etc.). The religious group consisted of Ultra-Orthodox Jews (n=63) and the non-religious group was made up of Secular Jews (n=86). Both intrusive and avoidance symptoms of PTSD were significantly lower among Ultra-Orthodox Jews compared to Secular Jews (p<0.01); however, when the age of participants and years of body handling were controlled for, significant differences disappeared.

Solomon et al (2005) also examined the relationship between religiosity (coping by faith in God) and PTSD or acute stress symptoms in their survey of 512 community-dwelling adults in Israel (87% Jewish). Coping by faith in God was correlated with more stress symptoms (B=0.10, p<0.01). These findings contrasted with those of a survey of 533 religious and public high school Jewish students in Jerusalem by Schiff (2006). He compared religious students (Orthodox, n=212) and non-religious students (Conservative or Secular, n=324) on PTSD symptoms (20-item SRQ). Regression analyses indicated significantly fewer PTSD symptoms in religious students (B=-2.97, p=0.015), independent of other predictors of PTSD. Furthermore, among non-religious students, exposure to terrorism was positively correlated with PTSD symptoms (p<0.0001), while no association was found in religious students.

Similarly, in the study of 37 Israeli Jewish community-dwelling adults (15 exposed to terrorism, 22 controls), Gigi et al (2007) found that religiosity (5-item scale) was inversely associated with state anxiety (STAI) in the 15 participants exposed to terrorism (r=-0.68, p=0.008), but no association was found in the non-exposed control group (r=0.03, p=ns). Both studies above suggest that religious involvement buffers against the negative effects of terrorism on PTSD symptoms and anxiety.

In one of the largest studies to date, Laufer and Solomon (2006) analyzed data on 2,999 Jewish adolescents exposed to terrorist attacks in Israel, examining the relationship between PTSD symptoms and religiosity (Ultra-Orthodox=1, Secular=4). Although no association was found between religiosity and PTSD symptoms, those who were more religious experienced significantly greater *post-traumatic growth* compared to those who were less religious (B=-0.16, p<0.001). In a later report on the same sample, though, Laufer and Solomon (2009) also found no association between intrinsic religiosity (assessed by a 14-item Gorsuch-McPherson scale) and PTSD symptoms.

In one of the few experimental studies, Chen (2006) compared changes in anxiety (STAI) in a sample of prisoners in Israel (71% Jewish) who participated in either a spiritual treatment group or a non-spiritual group during a 6-12 month period. The spiritual group (n=43) participated in a 12-step program that focused on "believing in and submitting oneself to a higher power, seeking to improve conscious contact with this higher power through prayer and meditation, and using one's spiritual awakening to carry this message to others still suffering from addiction," while others (n=50) participated in a group that did not stress these religious/spiritual elements (non-randomized). Results indicated a greater reduction in anxiety scores among those in the 12-step spiritual group compared to the other group (F = 5.52, p < 0.05).

In the largest study to date, Shmueli and Tamir (2007) surveyed a random sample of 3,056 urban-dwelling Jewish adults in Israel, comparing stress levels (assessed by a single item ranging from 1-4) with degree of religiosity (assessed by a single item ranging 1 to 4 from Ultra-Orthodox to Secular). Ultra-Orthodox and religious participants were nearly 40% less likely to report they felt stressed compared to Secular Jews, controlling for multiple characteristics using logistic regression (OR=0.62, 95% CI=0.49-0.79).

In one of the few studies that has examined the relationship between religiosity and anxiety in medical patients, Goldzweig and colleagues (2009) surveyed 339 Israeli patients with colorectal cancer. They found that a 3-item measure of religious/spiritual support was unrelated to a subscale assessing anxious preoccupation in analyses stratified by marital status and gender (although stratifying in this manner may have reduced the power to detect a difference).

In a study discussed earlier, Rosmarin et al (2009a) found no difference in trait anxiety (STAI) between Orthodox Jews (n=141), non-Orthodox Jews (n=93), and Protestants (n=97) in Canada. However, religious beliefs (12-item scale) and religious practices (4-item scale) were both inversely related to trait anxiety in Orthodox Jews (r=-0.34, p<0.001 and -0.27, p<0.01, respectively). No relationship, however, was found in non-Orthodox Jews or in Protestants. In the second study by Rosmarin et al (2009b) discussed earlier, they surveyed 354 community-dwelling adults in the U.S. and Canada, finding no difference on measures of worry or anxiety between religious groups (Hasidic, Yeshiva Orthodox, Modern Orthodox, Conservative, Reform, other Jewish, Catholics, mainline Protestants, Evangelical Protestants, and Mormon). However, in the overall sample (66% Jewish), religiosity measured by a 5-item general religiousness scale, a 4-item religious practices scale, and a 24-item trust/mistrust in God scale, was inversely related to worry on the Penn scale (r's ranging from -0.17 to -0.25, p<0.01) and inversely related to trait anxiety on the STAI (r's ranging from -0.17 to -0.21, p<0.01). These associations remained significant after controlling for age and whether or not the participant was in treatment.

Recent Research

All studies described above (except Chen, 2006) were cross-sectional in design, preventing speculation on direction of causation in these relationships (i.e., did religiosity affect anxiety, or did anxiety affect religiosity). Only a randomized clinical trial (RCT) can determine the direction of causation. Rosmarin and colleagues (2010) conducted an RCT via the Internet to examine the effects of a spiritually-integrated treatment (SIT) on subclinical anxiety in Jews. Participants were randomized to SIT (n=36), progressive muscle relaxation (PMR, n=42), or a waitlist control group (WLC, n=47). The overall sample was 65.6% Orthodox, 48.4% of whom were Ultra-Orthodox. The SIT intervention included components that were cognitive (reading inspiring stories and excerpts from Jewish religious literature) and behavioral (spiritual exercises to increase gratitude and prayer). Perceived stress scale (PSS) and Penn worry (PSWQ) scores were the primary outcomes assessed at baseline (T0), 2 weeks (immediately post-treatment, T1), and 6 weeks (post-treatment, T2). Results indicated that the group by time interaction from T1 to T3 was significant for both perceived stress (F=5.8, p<0.005) and worry (F=12.2, p<0.001), with the lowest scores recorded for the SIT group. While not definitive, this suggests that religious involvement among Jews may cause a reduction in worry and anxiety symptoms.

Summary

Numerous studies have examined anxiety among Jews. Two studies compared anxiety (STAI) in Jews and non-Jews in U.S. and Canada, finding no difference. Sixteen studies examined religiosity and anxiety in Jews, including a non-randomized clinical trial and a randomized clinical trial that tested religious/spiritual interventions. Most studies (13 of 16) were conducted in Israel. Of the 14 cross-sectional studies, 6 (43%) found lower anxiety in Jews who were more religious (two showing that religiosity buffered against the effects of trauma on PTSD symptoms in high school students and adults). Both clinical trials reported that religious/spiritual interventions significantly reduced anxiety symptoms compared to active control interventions. Four 14 studies (29%) found higher anxiety among religious Jews, two of those finding that an increase in religiosity since childhood was associated with higher OCD symptoms in Israeli Jews (although OCD measures may have been confounded by indicators of conservative religious beliefs). Three of 14 studies found no association and one study reported mixed results. In the two largest studies, one found greater post-traumatic growth in religious Israeli adolescents exposed to terrorism and the other found lower stress levels in Israeli adults who were more religious.

8 SUBSTANCE USE AND ABUSE

Drinking alcohol is not forbidden in Judaism, as long as it is done in moderation (use of illicit drugs, however, is not endorsed by any Jewish tradition). Alcoholism has long been known to be relatively infrequent among Jews (Blacker, 1966). Jews (like East Asians) have a lower tolerance for alcohol due to genetic factors. Research indicates that 20% of Jews have a gene variant that protects them from alcoholism (alcohol dehydrogenase 1b) by increasing levels of acetaldehyde that is toxic, causing headaches, nausea and flushing (Hasin et al., 2002).

Past Research

In one of the first studies to compare Jews and non-Jews on alcohol use, Knupfer and Room (1967) surveyed 1,212 persons in the San Francisco Bay area with Irish or Jewish names identified systematically in a 1962 Oakland telephone directory. They found Irish Catholics drank more than White Protestants, who drank more than Jews (36% vs 26% vs 18% drinking nearly every day). Orthodox Jews were less likely to drink that non-affiliated Jews, and Jews overall were less likely to approve drinking or condone intoxication. Two additional studies (not included in our 2012 systematic review) compared substance use among Jews and non-Jews in the early 1970s. One study of 551 adolescents (86% Jewish) attending Jewish secondary schools in New York City found that Christians were more involved in alcohol and illicit drug use than Jews (Milman & Su 1973). The second report (unpublished) from

Toronto, Canada, also conducted in adolescents, found more substance use among Jews and those with no religious background than among Christians (Smart et al. 1970).

More recently, Levav et al (1997) examined a random sample of 5772 U.S. adults, finding that alcohol abuse/dependence among non-Jewish males was over four times that of Jewish males for current disorders (OR 4.11, 95% CI 1.84-9.20) and nearly three times greater for lifetime disorders (OR 2.82, 95% CI 1.72-4.60). In the only prospective cohort study to date on Jews and substance use, Moore et al (1990) examined 1,014 male medical students enrolled at Johns Hopkins from 1948 to 1964 and followed up through 1986. They found that alcohol abuse on follow-up (scores of 2 or higher on CAGE scale indicating four or more alcoholic drinks/day) was predicted by *non-Jewish* ancestry (RR=3.1, 95% CI 1.4-6.9), an effect that remained significant after controlling for lack of religious affiliation, history of a problem caused by drinking, smoking, history of maternal mental illness/alcoholism, nonsocial use of alcohol, and anxiety.

Finally, analyzing data from a random sample of 9,282 community dwelling adults participating in the US National Comorbidity Survey, Degenhardt et al (2007) found that Jews (n=88) were 50% less likely to use alcohol (OR=0.5, 95% CI 0.2-1.5), but 30% more likely to use cannabis (OR=1.3, 95% CI 0.8-2.1) and 60% more likely to use cocaine (OR=1.6, 95% CI 0.8-3.4), compared to mainline Protestants. None of these differences, however, were statistically significant due to the small number of Jews. In the U.S. National Alcohol Survey of 7,370 adults, Michalak et al (2007) found that Jews (n=130) were the least likely to say that alcohol should be prohibited (16.3%), but were also the least likely to be heavy drinkers (12.5%). Jews were also almost 70% less likely to be heavy drinkers than to be moderate drinkers (OR=0.31, 95% CI 0.15-0.62, p=0.004).

Recent Research

Three other more recent studies give a sense of what has been reported in the literature since 2010. Neumark and Bar-Hamburger (2011) analyzed data from the 2009 Israeli National School Study, which surveyed a nationally representative sample of 7,166 youth ages 12-18 (75% Jewish and 25% Arab). The focus of this report was volatile substance misuse. No significant difference was found between Jewish and Arabic youth in past-month use of inhalants (OR=0.94, 95% CI 0.7-1.3) nor did inhalant use vary by religious orthodoxy (OR=1.05, 95% 0.8-1.3).

In the second study, Laufer et al (2013) analyzed data from a survey of 2,948 consecutive patients attending six primary care clinics in Israel examining the prevalence and predictors of mental disorder. Mental disorders were diagnosed using a structured psychiatric interview, the World Health Organization's CIDI. Participants were divided into secular (those without religious belief or observance, 53%), traditional (those who observed key festivals and laws, 39%), and religious (those with a high degree of religious belief and observance, 7%). The prevalence of alcohol dependence (0.3%) and alcohol abuse (0.4%) in the overall sample was quite low. Although substance use disorders were not specifically examined by degrees of religious observance, the prevalence of "any" mental disorder did not significantly vary across categories of religious observance (OR=0.64, 95% CI 0.27-1.55 for religious vs. secular; OR=1.49, 95% CI 0.88-2.53 for traditional vs. secular). Degrees of religious observance also did not distinguish those with three or more mental disorders.

Finally, Isralowitz and Reznik (2015) surveyed 345 male adolescents attending three secular and three religious high schools in Israel. Lifetime and past month alcohol use was significantly lower among the 177 youth from religious schools compared to the 168 attending secular schools (lifetime: 54.9% vs. 74.5%, p<0.001; past month: 42.3% vs. 58.9%, p<0.01). Furthermore, when religiosity was assessed based on the categories secular (31.0% of sample), somewhat religious (34.2%), and religious (34.8%), higher levels of religiosity were associated with lower lifetime and past month use of alcohol (as well as with less binge drinking, less school underachievement, less violence, and less weapons possession).

Summary

Only a few studies have examined substance use/abuse among Jews, and there are genetic reasons why Jews may avoid the use and abuse of alcohol. Eight studies have compared Jews and non-Jews (seven from the U.S. or Canada), with four (50%) finding significantly less substance use/abuse in Jews compared to non-Jews, three finding no difference, and one reporting greater drug use in Jews. Three studies (all from Israel) examined the relationship between religiosity and substance use/abuse, with one finding an inverse relationship (for alcohol use among adolescents in religious and secular schools) and two reporting no association.

9 WELL-BEING AND HAPPINESS

Positive emotions include psychological well-being, happiness, satisfaction, hope, optimism, and having meaning and purpose in life. These are indicators of the positive side of emotions, in contrast to the negative (psychopathology). How do Jews fair in this regard?

Early Research
Studies conducted in the U.S. have not found a strong relationship between religiosity and well-being in Jews. Hadaway and Roof (1978) analyzed data from a national probability sample of 2,164 Americans participating in the Quality of American Life Survey. The purpose was to examine the relationship between religious involvement and the "worthwhileness of life" (assessed by a single item ranging from 1=useless to 7=worthwhile). In the overall sample, importance of religious faith, church/synagogue membership, and frequency of religious attendance were all significantly correlated with "worthwhileness of life" (p<.001); importance of faith was the strongest predictor in a model that included number of friends, marital status, age, education, health, income, and race. However, among the 64 Jews in the sample, no relationship was found between any religious variable and worthwhileness of life (r's ranging from -0.11 to 0.02); low power due to the small number of Jews may have influenced the lack of significant findings, although the small size of the correlations and direction of association (negative) suggest otherwise.

Analyzing data from a random sample of 34,706 community

dwelling U.S. adults (including 748 Jews), Ferriss (2002) also found little variation in happiness between Jews, Protestants and Catholics, although Jews were slightly more likely to indicate that they were "not too happy" (14.2% of Jews vs. 11.6% of Catholics and 11.8% of Protestants).

Cohen (2002) analyzed data from three studies, two involving Jews and all involving participants living in the U.S. In the first study, he analyzed data on 2,279 U.S. adults surveyed as part of the General Social Survey (1,527 Protestants, 705 Catholics, and 50 Jews). No difference was found in happiness between the three denominations; happiness, however, was associated with spirituality/religiosity in Christians (too few Jews were included to examine associations in that group). In the second study, Cohen analyzed data on a convenience sample of 94 Catholics, 95 Jews, and 120 Protestants (mean age of all groups was 33-34 years); again, no difference was found in happiness between the three religious groups. While measures of spirituality were strongly associated with life satisfaction in Catholics and Protestants, no association was found in Jews. Cohen concluded that spirituality/religiosity was more strongly associated with happiness/quality of life in Christians than in Jews, although only one of the three studies actually tested this hypothesis.

In contrast to studies among Jews in the U.S., those conducted among Jews in Israel are more likely to find a positive relationship between religiosity and well-being. Anson et al (1990a) examined the effects of religiosity on life satisfaction in 639 community dwelling Israeli Jewish adults age 60 or older assessed within two months of retirement, and followed participants for one year. Baseline religiosity (observance of religious rituals) predicted an increase in life satisfaction after one year. A decline in physical health or a decline in life satisfaction, in turn, predicted an increase in religiosity (likely as a coping response). In a second study, Anson and colleagues (1990b) surveyed a random sample of members of a "religious kibbutz" (n=105) and members of a "non-religious kibbutz" (n=125) in Israel. The kibbutzim were located in a similar region, were of similar size, and had both been established about 45 years previously. Recent negative life events were assessed with the 32-item Holms and Rahe scale, and psychological well-being was measured by the 6-item Scale of Psychological Distress (Ben-Sira). While recent life events predicted an increase in psychological distress among members of the non-religious kibbutz, no such relationship was found among members of the religious kibbutz (again indicating stress buffering). Shkolnik et al (2001) surveyed 60 older male adults in Israel, also finding that greater religious observance (religious vs. traditional) was positively correlated with life satisfaction.

Francis and Katz (2002) surveyed 298 female Jewish college students (58% Orthodox) in Israel examining the relationship between a measure of Jewish religiosity (24-item Attitude toward Judaism Scale) and the 29-item Oxford Happiness Inventory, finding a small positive correlation between the two after controlling for personality variables (B=0.11, p=0.05). In a separate study of 203 male college students at a religious university in Israel, Francis et al (2004) used the same measures and found similar but somewhat stronger findings (B=0.21, p=0.01). In a survey of 668 Jewish college students in Israel (51% Secular, 20% Traditional, 29% Religious), Vilchinsky and Kravetz (2005) found that an 18-item measure of religious practices and beliefs (Ben-Meir & Kedem, 1979) was positively correlated with psychological well-being measured using the Mental Health Inventory. This positive association was found in Religious and Secular Jews (mediated by meaning in life), but not in Traditional Jews.

Mot all studies of Jews in Israel report a positive link between religiosity and well-being. Isecovich (2001) examined the relationship between religiosity (assessed by the Ben-Meir & Kedem, 1979) and psychological well-being (assessed by the 17-item Philadelphia Geriatric Center Morale Scale) in 464 female residents of 48 old age homes in Israel. No association was found between religiosity and well-being after adjusting for control variables. Billig and colleagues (2006) surveyed a systematically identified sample of 267 Israeli adults living in the Gaza Strip who were being forced to move out of their homes because of a government order to relocate elsewhere. Scores on a 4-item indicator of religious coping were not associated with life satisfaction. However, religious coping was inversely associated with overall distress after controlling for covariates (B=-0.12, p=0.02).

Recent Research

Two studies are summarized here to give a sense of what recent research has reported. Analyzing data from the World Values Survey,

Levin (2012) examined the relationship between well-being and religious involvement among 1,023 Jews living in Israel and 859 Jews living outside of Israel. Well-being was measured using two single-item measures of happiness and life satisfaction. Religious involvement was assessed with six measures, including importance of God in life and frequency of attendance at synagogue. Results differed depending on whether Jews were residing in or outside Israel. For Jews in Israel, importance of God in life was associated with greater life satisfaction ($\beta=0.07$, $p<0.05$), but not greater happiness; for Jews living outside Israel, both importance of God in life and frequency of attendance at synagogue were related to greater happiness ($\beta=0.13$, $p<0.01$ and $\beta=0.14$, $p<0.01$, respectively), but not to greater life satisfaction.

Finally, Dilmaghani (2017) compared religiosity and well-being across religious groups using data from the Ethnic Diversity Survey of Statistics Canada, which surveyed a national random sample of 41,695 Canadian adults ages 15 to 65. Religious affiliations were Catholic (42%), Protestant (27%), none (16%), other religion (13%), Muslim (2%), and Jewish (1%). Religiosity was assessed by importance of religion in life, frequency of religious attendance, and frequency of private religious practices, creating a Composite Religiosity Index (CRI) that ranged from 0 to 15. Subjective well-being was assessed by a single question that examined overall satisfaction with life on a 1-5 scale, although categories were collapsed into being "very satisfied with life" vs. other. Results indicated that Muslims scored highest on religiosity (CRI=9.3) and lowest on annual income; in contrast, Jews scored lowest on religiosity (CRI=7.2), but highest on annual income. Catholic, Protestant, Muslim, and other religious affiliations were associated with being "very satisfied with life," compared to those with no religious affiliation. No difference in life satisfaction, however, was found between Jews and those with no affiliation. In Catholics, Protestants and Muslims, importance of religion was significantly and positively related to greater life satisfaction (after multiple controls), whereas greater private religious activity was (surprisingly) related to lower life satisfaction. Among Jews, no religious variables were associated with life satisfaction either positively or negatively, similar to the trend mentioned in earlier studies conducted in North America.

Summary

Fourteen studies were reviewed that examined positive emotions/ psychological well-being in Jews. Of the 12 studies that examined religiosity, eight (57%, all conducted among Jews living in Israel) found a positive relationship between religiosity and well-being, and four reported no association (33%, all conducted among Jews living in the U.S. or Canada). Three studies also compared Jews and non-Jews on psychological well-being, all finding similar levels, with the exception of one study reporting that the response "not to happy" was slightly higher in Jews and one study reporting that life satisfaction was similar in Jews and those with no religious affiliation (both studies from the U.S.). Thus, for Jews living in the U.S., there is little evidence that religiosity is related to psychological well-being; however, greater religiosity is consistently related to more positive emotions and greater well-being among Jews living in Israel.

10 CLINICAL APPLICATIONS

In this chapter, I provide five recommendations that mental health professionals, pastoral counselors, and clergy may find useful when caring for Jewish clients or members of their congregation. But first, let us examine a case vignette.

Case Vignette

> Rachel is a 40 year-old recently divorced Jewish woman living in New York City who comes in to see a non-Jewish psychologist for help in treating her depression that has been resistant to several courses of antidepressants. During her initial evaluation, the therapist takes a spiritual history and learns that while she was raised in a Jewish home and used to attend the local Conservative synagogue regularly, she stopped attending after her divorce 12 months ago. She says that she is angry at God for allowing the marriage to fall apart, and feels uncomfortable seeing her old friends at the synagogue. She has become quite isolated since then, spending most of her time either at work or watching TV at home during the week and on most weekends. Both of her children are away at college and she sees them only during school breaks and occasionally on weekends. She has few friends and has little motivation to develop new relationships, especially the way she has been feeling lately. The therapist begins a course of cognitive-behavioral

therapy to treat her depression. During the fourth session, after a therapeutic relationship has been established, the therapist asks Rachel about the possibility of her re-establishing a connection with her synagogue (or a different synagogue in the area, if she is concerned about couples she and her husband used to associate with). With gentle persistent encouragement from her therapist, Rachel eventually relents and agrees to try attending synagogue again (but a different one than previously). Three months later, with coaching from her therapist, Rachel has established new relationships with members at the synagogue (including a male friend that she met there), and her depressive symptoms have significantly improved.

The case above illustrates the impact that reconnecting with the Jewish community may have in the treatment of a Jewish patient with a depressive disorder. The therapist was guided by an initial spiritual history, and after a therapeutic relationship had been established, proceeded gently and at the patient's own pace. The following are recommended for therapists and clergy who seek to help Jewish clients or members of a congregation.

1. <u>Take a Spiritual History</u>. Given the different branches of Judaism and wide range of belief and practice, the first recommendation is to take a careful and detailed spiritual history (Koenig, 2013). Does the person consider himself or herself a secular or cultural Jew (no religious affiliation) or do they have religious ties (reform/traditional, conservative/religious, or Orthodox/Ultra-Orthodox)? If the person indicates that he or she is secular and only engages in religious activities as a cultural practice, then there is no need to continue with the spiritual history (although it might be helpful to determine if the person has always been secular, whether a change occurred from religious to secular, and why). If religious, what religious beliefs and practices are particularly important to them? Is the he or she connected to the Jewish religious community and how close is this connection? Are religious beliefs used to cope with stressful life situations, and how effective are they in relieving distress? If the person is religious and religious beliefs have been helpful, is he or she open to a religious approach to therapy (see below), or at a minimum,

might they be receptive to the therapist utilizing their religious beliefs and practices as resources to help them cope? Finally, ask if the person thinks that their Jewish beliefs are in any way interfering with their mental health or contributing to mental health problems. The latter question should be asked in a way that does not challenge the person's beliefs or imply that those beliefs are contributing to the problem (see #5 below).

2. <u>Screen for Depression or OCD Symptoms</u>. Given the increased rate of depression among Jews compared to non-Jews, a high index of suspicion should be maintained for significant depressive symptoms. In addition, the person's religious beliefs concerning suicide should be explored (acceptable, unacceptable). This is particularly important in Jews who describe themselves as secular or not religious. Orthodox Jews, given the many rituals that are normative, should also be screened for obsessive thoughts and practices that may go beyond what is normative for the Orthodox tradition and extend into other areas of daily life (hoarding, checking, handwashing, etc.).

3. <u>Support Religious Beliefs/Practices</u>. Since the majority of studies indicate that religious involvement is associated with better mental health in Jews, it is reasonable to consider supporting those beliefs and practices unless obviously pathological. For example, as in the case above, one might encourage involvement in the Jewish community to help to increase social connections and reduce isolation and loneliness. Encouraging involvement with others in celebration of Jewish holidays and feasts may serve the same purpose. Never, however, attempt to coerce a person to believe or practice in a certain manner. The therapist or clergy helper should always proceed at the client's own pace and keep the treatment centered on the client's religious beliefs (or lack of belief).

4. <u>Consider Religious Psychotherapy</u>. If the client is willing or prefers a religious approach to treatment, consider either referral to a Jewish mental health professional or rabbi who provides treatment from this perspective, or think about administering a form of religious cognitive-behavioral therapy (CBT) that addresses depressive or anxiety symptoms. An evidence-based religious form

of CBT has been developed and shown to be similar in effectiveness to standard secular CBT (especially in those who are more religious) (Koenig et al., 2015). A Jewish version of this manualized intervention is readily available without cost, along with therapist and client workbooks (and a brief training video) (CSTH, 2014).

5. Always Respect Beliefs. Whether or not religious psychotherapy (or a less systematic use of the client's Jewish beliefs and practices) is being considered, the therapist should always be respectful of the person's Jewish beliefs and rituals. As noted above, religious interventions should always be client-centered (not centered on the therapist's or clergy's beliefs) and directed by a thorough spiritual history (Koenig & Al Zaben, 2017). Even when religious beliefs or practices are used in pathological ways that seem to generate or maintain illness, it is important to proceed cautiously when challenging or trying to alter such beliefs/practices. Always seek guidance from those who are knowledgeable about the client's Jewish beliefs and practices (e.g., rabbi with mental health training from the client's branch of Judaism).

10 SUMMARY AND CONCLUSIONS

Jews make up a small proportion of the world population (0.2%), but have had a tremendous impact on medicine and psychiatry. Over 80% of Jews live either in Israel or the U.S., so mental health professionals and clergy from these two countries are likely to encounter Jewish clients. The primary Jewish Scriptures are the Torah, the Navi-im, and the Ketuvim (which together make up the Hebrew Bible) and the Talmud (historical commentaries by Jewish scholars on these Scriptures). There are four major branches of Judaism in the United States (Secular, Reform, Conservative, and Orthodox) and four similar branches in Israel (Secular, Traditional, Religious, Ultra-Orthodox). The 13 principles of the Jewish faith have been summarized by Maimonides, which also tend to be emphasized by some modern Jewish theologians (although there is considerable debate between Jewish branches on how authoritative these principles are today). Jewish beliefs and practices vary in frequency among Jews in the U.S., and this is also true for Jews in Israel, again depending heavily on the particular Jewish branch a person is affiliated with.

Many Jewish beliefs and communal practices have implications for mental health. Systematic research shows that Jews (particularly those in Israel and those from Orthodox branches) frequently use religion to cope with life stressors. Jews experience more depressive symptoms and disorders than non-Jews, at least in studies conducted in the U.S. and Canada. Despite this, 75% of studies (6/8) report less depression among Jews who are more religious, especially studies in

Orthodox Jews. This suggests that there may be a higher prevalence of depression in Secular Jews. Research on suicide is more equivocal (three studies finding higher and three studies finding lower suicide rates/attempts in Jews compared to non-Jews), although religious adolescents in Israel appear to hold more negative attitudes toward suicide.

Concerning studies on anxiety, 43% (6/14) of cross-sectional studies report lower anxiety among Jews who are more religious, and 29% (4/14) find greater anxiety (two reporting increased OCD symptoms) in the more religious. Most of these studies were conducted among Israeli Jews. In the two largest studies, post-traumatic growth was significantly higher and stress level significantly lower in religious Israeli Jews. Two studies report that religiosity buffers the effects of terrorism in adult and adolescent Jews. Two clinical trials have found that religious/spiritual interventions significantly reduced anxiety symptoms compared to active control interventions. When anxiety levels in Jews are compared to those in non-Jews in the U.S. and Canada, no differences have been found.

Substance use/abuse is generally lower in Jews than in non-Jews, and greater religious involvement tends to be associated with less substance use/abuse, at least among youth attending religious and secular schools in Israel. Psychological well-being is similar in Jews and non-Jews, although higher religiosity is associated with greater well-being in the majority of studies (8 of 12), and no studies find lower well-being in more religious Jews. Finally, Jews are also more likely than non-Jews to see mental health professionals for psychiatric problems, and more likely to be mental health professionals themselves.

In conclusion, research indicates that Jews in Israel tend to be more religious than those in the North America, and in North America, Jews experience more depression than non-Jews. However, greater religiosity is associated with less depression and greater well-being in the majority of studies whether conducted in North America or Israel (although especially Israel). This, together with randomized clinical trials of religious/spiritual interventions showing benefit, suggests that Jewish religious beliefs and practices are mental health resources that can be tapped into for health and healing. A careful spiritual history should be taken on all Jewish persons to identify religious beliefs and practices that are important to them, realizing that these are often utilized to cope with stress and can be integrated into psychotherapeutic treatments if the person is open to or prefers this approach.

REFERENCES

Amit BH, Krivoy A, Mansbach-Kleinfeld I, Zalsman G, Ponizovsky AM, Hoshen M, Farbstein I, Apter A, Weizman A, Shoval G (2014). Religiosity is a protective factor against self-injurious thoughts and behaviors in Jewish adolescents: findings from a nationally representative survey. *European Psychiatry* 29(8):509-513

Anson, O., Antonovsky, A., & Sagy, S. (1990a). Religiosity and well-being among retirees: A question of causality. *Behavior, Health, and Aging,* 1, 85-97.

Anson, O., Carmel, S., Bonneh, D.Y., Levenson, A., Maoz, B. (1990b). Recent life events, religiosity, and health: An individual or collective effect. *Human Relations* 43, 1051-1066.

Bailey, W. T., & Stein, L. B. (1995). Jewish affiliation in relation to suicide rates. *Psychological Reports,* 76(2), 561-562

Ben-Meir, Y., & Kedem, P. (1979). Index of religiosity of the Jewish population of Israel. *Megamot,* 24, 353-362

Bergin AE, Jensen JP (1990). Religiosity of psychotherapists: A national survey. *Psychotherapy* 27:3-7

Billig, M., Kohn, R., & Levav, I. (2006). Anticipatory stress in the population facing forced removal from the Gaza Strip. *Journal of Nervous & Mental Disease* 194(3):195-200

Blacker, E. (1966). Sociocultural factors in alcoholism. *International Psychiatry Clinics,* 3 (2), 51-80

Central Bureau of Statistics (2016). 68th Independence Day - 8.5 million residents in the State of Israel. *Israeli Central Bureau of Statistics.* Retrieved from http://www.cbs.gov.il/reader/?MIval=cw_usr_view_SHTML&ID=705 (accessed on 2/28/17)

Chen, G. (2006). Social support, spiritual program, and addiction recovery. *International Journal of Offender Therapy & Comparative Criminology,* 50(3), 306-323.

Cohen, A. B. (2002). The importance of spirituality in well-being for Jews and Christians. *Journal of Happiness Studies, 3*(3), 287-310.

Cohen, M., Azaiza, F. (2007). Health-promoting behaviors and health locus of control from a multicultural perspective. *Ethnicity & Disease* 17(4), 636-642.

Cooklin, R.S., Ravindran, A., & Carney, M.W.P. (1983). The patterns of mental disorder in Jewish and non-Jewish admissions to a district general hospital psychiatric unit: Is manic-depressive illness a typically Jewish disorder? *Psychological Medicine,* 13, 209-212.

CSTH (2014). *Religiously-Integrated Cognitive Behavioral Therapy (RCBT) Manuals and Workbooks* (including training video). Durham, NC: Duke University Center for Spirituality, Theology and Health. Retrieved from http://www.spiritualityandhealth.duke.edu/index.php/religious-cbt-study/therapy-manuals (accessed on 3/1/17)

CSTH (2010-2017). *Crossroads.* Durham, North Carolina: Duke University Center for Spirituality, Theology and Health. Retrieved from https://spiritualityandhealth.duke.edu/index.php/publications/crossroads (accessed on 3/1/17)

Danto, B. L., & Danto, J. M. (1983). Jewish and non-Jewish suicide in Oakland County, Michigan. *Crisis,* 4, 33-60.

Degenhardt, L., Chiu, W. T., Sampson, N., Kessler, R. C., & Anthony, J. C. (2007). Epidemiological patterns of extra-medical drug use in the United States: Evidence from the National Comorbidity Survey Replication, 2001-2003. *Drug and Alcohol Dependence, 90*(2-3), 210-223.

Delaney HD, Miller WR, Bisono AM (2013). Religiosity and spirituality among psychologists: a survey of clinician members of the American Psychological Association. *Spirituality in Clinical Practice* 1(S):95-106

Dilmaghani, M. (2017). Religiosity and subjective well-being in Canada. *Journal of Happiness Studies*, Jan 3, E-pub ahead of print (doi:10.1007/s10902-016-9837-7)

Dimitrovsky HZ (2001). Talmud and Midrash. *Encyclopedia Britannica.* Retrieved from https://www.britannica.com/topic/Talmud (accessed on 2/17/17)

Dubow, E. F., Pargament, K. I., Boxer, P., & Tarakeshwar, N. (2000). Initial investigation of Jewish early adolescents' ethnic identity, stress and coping. *Journal of Early Adolescence, 20*(4), 418-441.

Edland, J.F., Duncan, C.E. (1973). Suicide notes in Monroe County: A 23 year look (1950-1972). *Journal of Forensic Sciences*, 364-369

Encyclopedia Britannica (2008). Reform Judaism. *Encyclopedia Britannica.* Retrieved from https://www.britannica.com/topic/Reform-Judaism (accessed on 3/2/17)

Encyclopedia Britannica (1998a). Conservative Judaism. *Encyclopedia Britannica.* Retrieved from https://www.britannica.com/topic/Conservative-Judaism (accessed on 3/2/17)

Encyclopedia Britannica (1998b). Orthodox Judaism. *Encyclopedia Britannica.* Retrieved from https://www.britannica.com/topic/Orthodox-Judaism (accessed on 3/2/17)

Feinson MC, Meir A (2015). Exploring the mental health consequences of childhood abuse and the relevance of religiosity. *Journal of Interpersonal Violence* 30(3):499-521

Ferriss, A. L. (2002). Religion and the quality of life. *Journal of Happiness Studies, 3*(3), 199-215.

Figelman, M. (1968). A comparison of affective and paranoid disorders in Negroes and Jews. *International Journal of Social Psychiatry,* 14, 277-281.

Flics, D.H., & Herron, W.G. (1991). Activity-withdrawal, diagnosis, and demographics as predictors of premorbid adjustment. *Journal of Clinical Psychology,* 47, 189-196.

Florian, V., & Kravetz, S. (1983). Fear of personal death: attribution, structure, and relation to religious belief. *Journal of Personality and Social Psychology,* 44, 600-607.

Francis, L. J., & Katz, Y. J. (2002). Religiosity and happiness: A study among Israeli female undergraduates. *Research in the Social Scientific Study of Religion, 13,* 75-86.

Francis, L. J., Katz, Y. J., Yablon, Y., & Robbins, M. (2004). Religiosity, personality, and happiness: A study among Israeli male undergraduates. *Journal of Happiness Studies* 5(4) : 315-333.

Garfinkel, B., Froese, A., and Hood, J.(1982). Suicide attempts in children and adolescents. *American Journal of Psychiatry,* 139, 1257-1261.

Gargas, S. (1932). Suicide in the Netherlands. *Journal of Sociology,* 37, 697-713.

Gigi, A., Papirovitz, M., & Hagit, M. (2007). Memory functioning following terror attack and the suggested immunization by religious faith. *Stress and Health, 23*(3), 199-204.

Goldzweig, G., Andritsch, E., Hubert, A. Walach, N., Perry, S., Brenner, B., Baider, L. (2009). How relevant is marital status and gender variables in coping with colorectal cancer? A sample of middle-aged and older cancer survivors. *Psycho-Oncology* 18, 866-874

Goodman, M., Rubinstein, R.L., Alexander, B.B., & Lubersky (1991). Cultural differences among elderly women in coping with the death of an adult child. *Journal of Gerontology: Social Sciences*, 6, S321-S329.

Greenberg, D., & Shefler, G. (2002). Obsessive compulsive disorder in ultra-orthodox Jewish patients: A comparison of religious and non-religious symptoms. *Psychology and Psychotherapy: Theory, Research and Practice, 75*(2), 123-130.

Hadaway, C.K., & Roof, W.C. (1978). Religious commitment and the quality of life in American society. *Review of Religious Research*, 19, 295-307

Hasin, D., Aharonovich, E., Liu, X., Mamman, Z., Matseoane, K., Carr, L., & Li, T. K. (2002). Alcohol and ADH2 in Israel: Ashkenazis, Sephardics, and recent Russian immigrants. *American Journal of Psychiatry, 159*(8), 1432-1434.

Hermesh, H., Masser-Kavitzky, R., & Gross-Isseroff, R. (2003). Obsessive-compulsive disorder and Jewish religiosity. *Journal of Nervous & Mental Disease, 191*(3), 201-203.

Holzer J (editor and translator) (1901). *Moses Maimunis Einleitung zu Chelek* (including Introduction to Perek Helek*)*. Berlin: M. Poppelauer

Hyman, O. (2005). Religiosity and secondary traumatic stress in Israeli-Jewish body handlers. *Journal of Traumatic Stress, 18*(5), 491-495.

Iecovich, E. (2001). Religiousness and subjective well-being among Jewish female residents of old age homes in Israel. *Journal of Religious Gerontology, 13*(1), 31-46.

Isralowitz, R., & Reznik, A. (2015). Impact of religious education and religiosity on adolescent alcohol use and risk-taking behavior. *Religious Education, 110*(3), 303-310.

Kellner MM (1980). *Rabbi Isaac Abravanel on Maimonides' Principles of Faith*. Tradition 18(4): 343-356

Kellner MM (1987). Heresy and the nature of faith in medieval Jewish philosophy. *The Jewish Quarterly Review* 77(4):299-318

Kennedy, G.J., Kelman, H.R., Thomas, C., & Chen, J. (1996). The relation of religious preference and practice to depressive symptoms among 1,855 older adults. *Journal of Gerontology*, 51B, P301-P308.

Keshet Y, Liberman I (2014). Coping with illness and threat. Why non-religious Jews choose to consult rabbis on healthcare issues. *Journal of Religion and Health 53*(4), 1146-1160.

Knupfer, G., & Room, R. (1967). Drinking patterns and attitudes of Irish, Jewish, and white Protestant American men. *Quarterly Journal of Studies on Alcohol*, 28, 676-699.

Koenig HG, King DE, Carson VB (2012). *Handbook of Religion and Health*, 2nd ed. NY, NY: Oxford University Press

Koenig HG (2013). *Spirituality in Patient Care*, 3rd ed. Philadelphia, PA: Templeton Foundation Press

Koenig HG, Pearce MJ, Nelson B, Shaw SF, Robins CJ, Daher NS, Cohen HJ, Berk LS, Bellinger DL, Pargament KI, Rosmarin DH, Vasegh S, Kristeller J, Juthani N, Nies D, King MB (2015). Religious vs. conventional cognitive behavioral therapy for major depression in persons with chronic medical illness: A pilot randomized trial. *Journal of Nervous & Mental Disease* 203(4), 243-251.

Koenig HG, Al Zaben F (2017). Integrating Religious Faith into Patient Care: Commentary on…The Role of Faith in Mental Health Management: Philosophy, Psychology & Practice. *British Journal of Psychiatry Advances*, in press

Krumrei EJ, Pirutinsky S, Rosmarin DH (2013). Jewish spirituality, depression, and health: an empirical test of a conceptual framework. *International Journal of Behavioral Medicine* 20(3):327-336.

Laufer, A., & Solomon, Z. (2006). Posttraumatic symptoms and posttraumatic growth among Israeli youth exposed to terror incidents. *Journal of Social & Clinical Psychology, 25*(4), 429-447.

Laufer, A., Solomon, Z. (2009). Gender differences in PTSD in Israeli youth exposed to terror attacks. *Journal of Interpersonal Violence* 24, 959-976

Laufer, N., Zilber, N., Jecsmien, P., Maoz, B., Grupper, D., Hermesh, H., Gilad, R., Weizman, A., Munitz, H. (2013). Mental disorders in primary care in Israel: prevalence and risk factors. *Social Psychiatry and Psychiatric Epidemiology, 48*(10), 1539-1554.

Lester, D. (1996). Comment on "Jewish affiliation in relation to suicide rates." *Psychological Reports*, 78(3 pt 1), 834.

Levav, I, Kohn, R., Golding, J.M., & Weissman, M.M. (1997). Vulnerability of Jews to affective disorders. *American Journal of Psychiatry*, 154, 941-947

Levav, I., & Aisenberg, E. (1989). The epidemiology of suicide in Israel: international and intranational comparisons. *Suicide and Life-Threatening Behavior*, 19(2), 184-200.

Levin, J. (2012). Religion and positive well-being among Israeli and diaspora Jews: Findings from the World Values Survey. *Mental Health, Religion and Culture 15*(7): 709-720.

Lopez AD, Murray CC (1998). The global burden of disease, 1990–2020. *Nature Medicine* 4(11): 1241–1243

Malzberg, B. (1973). Mental disease among Jews in New York state, 1960-1961. *Acta Psychiatry Scandinavica*, 49, 479-518.

Michalak L, Trocki K, Bond J. (2007). Religion and alcohol in the U.S. National Alcohol Survey: how important is religion for abstention and drinking? *Drug and Alcohol Dependence* 87(2-3): 268-80.

Milman, D. H., & Su, W. (1973). Patterns of illicit drug and alcohol use among secondary school students. *Journal of Pediatrics, 83*, 314-320.

Moore, R.D., Mead, L., & Pearson, T.A. (1990). Youthful precursors of alcohol abuse in physicians. *American Journal of Medicine*, 88, 332-336.

Murray, C. & Lopez, A. (1996) *The Global Burden of Disease*. Cambridge, MA: Harvard University Press.

Neumark, Y., & Bar-Hamburger, R. (2011). Volatile substance misuse among youth in Israel: results of a national school survey. *Substance Use & Misuse, 46*(sup1), 21-26.

Petuchowski JJ (1998). *Studies in Modern Theology and Prayer* (pp 101-112). Philadelphia, PA: Jewish Publication Society

Pew Research Center (2012). The global religious landscape. *Pew Research Center: Religion & Public Life*. Retrieved from http://www.pewforum.org/2012/12/18/global-religious-landscape-exec/ (accessed on 2/17/17)

Pew Research Center (2013). A portrait of Jewish Americans. *Pew Research Center: Religion & Public Life*. Retrieved from http://www.pewforum.org/2013/10/01/jewish-american-beliefs-attitudes-culture-survey/ (accessed on 2/17/17)

Pew Research Center (2016a). Unlike U.S., few Jews in Israel identify as Reform or Conservative. *Pew Research Center: Religion & Public Life*. Retrieved from http://www.pewresearch.org/fact-tank/2016/03/15/unlike-u-s-few-jews-in-israel-identify-as-reform-or-conservative/ (accessed on 2/17/17)

Pew Research Center (2016b). Israel's religiously divided society. *Pew Research Center: Religion & Public Life*. Retrieved from http://www.pewforum.org/2016/03/08/israels-religiously-divided-society/ (accessed on 2/17/17)

Pirutinsky S, Rosmarin DH, Holt CL (2012). Religious coping moderates the relationship between emotional functioning and obesity. *Health Psychology* 31:394-397

Pirutinsky S, Rosmarin DH, Holt CL, Feldman RH, Caplan LS, Midlarsky E, Pargament KI (2011). Does social support mediate the moderating effect of intrinsic religiosity on the relationship between physical health and depressive symptoms among Jews? *Journal of Behavioral Medicine* 34:489-496

Rokach A, Chin J, Sha'ked A (2012). Religiosity and coping with loneliness. *Psychological Reports* 110(3): 731-742

Ronneberg CR, Miller EA, Dugan E, Porell F (2016). The protective effects of religiosity on depression: A 2-year prospective study. *The Gerontologist* 56 (3): 421-431

Rosenzweig, F. (2004). *Star of Redemption* (translated by Galli, BE). Madison, WI: University of Wisconsin Press

Rosmarin DH, Pargament KI, Pirutinsky S, Mahoney A (2010). A randomized controlled evaluation of a spiritually integrated treatment for subclinical anxiety in the Jewish community, delivered via the Internet. *Journal of Anxiety Disorders* 24(&):799-808

Rosmarin DH, Pirutinsky S, Green D, McKay D (2013). Attitudes toward spirituality/religion among members of the Association for Behavioral and Cognitive Therapies. *Professional Psychology: Research and Practice* 44(6):424-433.

Rosmarin, D.H., Pirutinsky, S., Pargament, K.I., Krumrei, E.J. (2009a). Are religious beliefs relevant to mental health among Jews? *Psychology of Religion and Spirituality* 1(3), 180-190

Rosmarin, D.H., Krumrei, E.J., Andersson, G. (2009b). Religion as a predictor of psychological distress in two religious communities. *Cognitive Behavior Therapy* 38, 54-64

Schiff, M. (2006). Living in the shadow of terrorism: Psychological distress and alcohol use among religious and non-religious adolescents in Jerusalem. *Social Sciences & Medicine*, 62 (9), 2301-2312.

Shapiro M (1993). Maimonides thirteen principles: The last word in Jewish theology? *The Torach U-Madda Journal* (Yeshiva University) 4 (Spring):187-242

Shkolnik, T., Weiner, C., Malik, L., & Festinger, Y. (2001). The effect of Jewish religiosity of elderly Israelis on their life satisfaction, health, function and activity. *Journal of Cross-Cultural Gerontology, 16*(3), 201-219.

Shmueli, A., & Tamir, D. (2007). Health behavior and religiosity among Israeli Jews. *Israel Medical Association Journal, 9*(10), 703-707.

Silverman GS, Johnson KA, Cohen AB (2016). To believe or not to believe, that is not the question: The complexity of Jewish beliefs about God. *Psychology of Religion and Spirituality* 8(2):119-130

Smart, R. G., Fejer, D., & White, W. J. (1970). The extent of drug use in metropolitan Toronto schools: A study of changes from 1968-1970. Toronto: Addiction Research Foundation.

Solomon, Z., Gelkopf, M., Bleich, A. (2005). Is terror gender-blind? Gender differences in reaction to terror events. *Social Psychiatry & Psychiatric Epidemiology, 40*(12), 947-954.

Springer, M. B., Newman, A., Weaver, A. J., Siritsky, N., Linderblatt, C., Flannelly, K. J., et al. (2003). Spirituality, depression, and loneliness among Jewish seniors residing in New York City. *Journal of Pastoral Care & Counseling, 57*(3), 305-318.

Stein, D., Witztum, E., Brom, D., DeNour, A.K., Elizer, A. (1992). The association between adolescents' attitudes toward suicide and their psychosocial background and suicidal tendencies. *Adolescence*, 27, 949-959.

Vilchinsky, N., & Kravetz, S. (2005). How are religious belief and behavior good for you? An investigation of mediators relating religion to mental health in a sample of Israeli Jewish students. *Journal for the Scientific Study of Religion, 44*, 459-471.

Wolpe D (2013). Worshippers, a love story: Understanding the Jewish people's relationship to God. *The Tablet*, September 11. Retrieved from http://www.tabletmag.com/jewish-life-and-religion/143228/jews-god-love-story (accessed on 2/20/17)

Yeung, P.P., & Greenwald, S. (1992). Jewish Americans and mental health: Results of the NIMH Epidemiologic Catchment Area study. *Social Psychiatry and Psychiatric Epidemiology*, 27, 292-297.

Zeidner, M., Hammer, A.L. (1992). Coping with missile attack: Resources, strategies, and outcomes. *Journal of Personality* 60: 709–746.

Zohar, A. H., Goldman, E., Calamary, R., & Mashiah, M. (2005). Religiosity and obsessive-compulsive behavior in Israeli Jews. *Behaviour Research and Therapy, 43*(7), 857-868.

Further Resources

Koenig HG (2016). *You Are My Beloved. Really?* Amazon: Create Space Publishing Platform

Levin J (2015). *Upon These Three Things: Jewish Perspectives on Loving God.* Waco, TX: ISR Books

ABOUT THE AUTHOR

Harold G. Koenig, M.D., M.H.Sc., completed his undergraduate education at Stanford University, nursing school at San Joaquin Delta College, medical school training at the University of California at San Francisco, and geriatric medicine, psychiatry, and biostatistics training at Duke University Medical Center. He is currently board certified in general psychiatry, and formerly boarded in family medicine, geriatric medicine, and geriatric psychiatry, and is on the faculty at Duke as Professor of Psychiatry and Behavioral Sciences, and Associate Professor of Medicine. He is also Adjunct Professor in the Department of Medicine at King Abdulaziz University, Jeddah, Saudi Arabia, and in the School of Public Health at Ningxia Medical University, Yinchuan, People's Republic of China. Dr. Koenig is Director of the Center for Spirituality, Theology and Health at Duke University Medical Center, and has published extensively in the fields of mental health, geriatrics, and religion, with over 500 scientific peer-reviewed articles and book chapters, and more than 40 books. His research on religion, health and ethical issues in medicine has been featured on dozens of national and international TV news programs (including ABC's World News Tonight, The Today Show, Good Morning America. Dr. Oz Show, and NBC Nightly News), over a hundred national or international radio programs, and hundreds of newspapers and magazines (including Reader's Digest, Parade Magazine, Newsweek, Time, and Guidepost). Dr. Koenig has given testimony before the U.S. Senate (1998) and U.S. House of Representatives (2008) concerning the benefits of religion and spirituality on public health, and travels widely to give seminars and workshops on this topic. He is the recipient of the 2012 Oskar Pfister Award from the American Psychiatric Association.

www.ingramcontent.com/pod-product-compliance
Lightning Source LLC
Chambersburg PA
CBHW070837310526
45788CB00017B/1469